Pangolin

by Laura Bryant

Consultant: Darin Collins, DVM
Director, Animal Health Programs
Woodland Park Zoo
Seattle, Washington

BEARPORT
PUBLISHING

New York, New York

Credits

Cover, © Daniel Haesslich/iStock; TOC, © 2630ben/Shutterstock; 4–5, © Pete Oxford/Minden Pictures; 6T, © Africa Studio/Shutterstock; 6B, © Katrina Elena/Shutterstock; 6–7, © Daniel Haesslich/iStock; 7T, © Frans Lanting/MINT Images/Science Source; 7B, © girishacf/iStock; 8–9, © Pete Oxford/Minden Pictures; 10, © Paul D Stewart/Nature Picture Library; 11T, © Peter Titmuss/Shutterstock; 11B, © dan_alto/iStock; 12T, © LeonP/Shutterstock; 12BL, © Jen Guyton/ Nature Picture Library; 12BR, © Jen Guyton/Nature Picture Library; 13, © Jen Guyton/Nature Picture Library; 14, © Klein & Hubert/Nature Picture Library; 15T, © schankz/Shutterstock; 15B, © PK6289/ iStock; 16T, © Roland Seitre/Nature Picture Library; 16B, © Klein & Hubert/Nature Picture Library; 17, © Scott Hurd/Alamy; 18–19, © DarrenBradleyPhotography/iStock; 20, © Suzi Eszterhas/ Minden Pictures; 21, © Suzi Eszterhas/Minden Pictures; 22 (T to B), © ANDREYGUDKOV/ iStock, © Dennis, David M./Animals Animals, and © Jinying Du/Dreamstime; 23TL, © Peter Titmuss/ Shutterstock; 23TR, © DieterMeyrl/iStock; 23BL, © Johannes Gerhardus Swanepoel/Dreamstime; 23BR, © 2630ben/Shutterstock.

Publisher: Kenn Goin
Senior Editor: Joyce Tavolacci
Creative Director: Spencer Brinker
Design: Debrah Kaiser
Photo Researcher: Thomas Persano

Library of Congress Cataloging-in-Publication Data

Names: Bryant, Laura, 1987– author.
Title: Pangolin / by Laura Bryant ; consultant Darin Collins, DVM, Director,
    Animal Health Programs, Woodland Park Zoo, Seattle, Washington.
Description: New York, New York : Bearport Publishing, [2018] | Series: Even
    weirder and cuter | Includes bibliographical
    references and index.
Identifiers: LCCN 2017034361 (print) | LCCN 2017045882 (ebook) |
ISBN 9781684025237 (ebook) | ISBN 9781684024650 (library)
Subjects: LCSH: Pangolins—Juvenile literature. | Endangered
    species—Juvenile literature.
Classification: LCC QL737.P5 (ebook) | LCC QL737.P5 B79 2018 (print) | DDC
    599.3/1—dc23
LC record available at https://lccn.loc.gov/2017034361

For more information, write to Bearport Publishing Company, Inc., 45 West 21st Street, Suite 3B, New York, New York 10010. Printed in the United States of America.

10 9 8 7 6 5 4 3 2 1

Contents

What's this weird
but cute animal?

It's a
pangolin.

4

HARD scales!

Tiny **ey**e**s**!

Big claws!

Some pangolins are
as small as toy poodles.

Others are as large
as golden retrievers.

long-tailed pangolin

Chinese pangolin

There are eight kinds of pangolins.

cape pangolin

Pangolins are **mammals.**

Yet, they don't have much fur or hair.

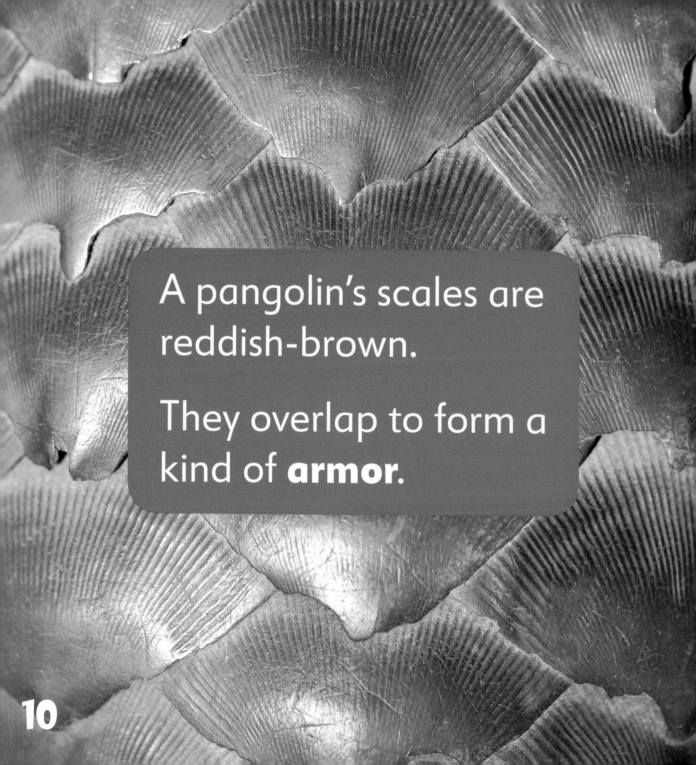

A pangolin's scales are reddish-brown.

They overlap to form a kind of **armor**.

Even the animal's head and tail are scaly!

The scales are made of the same stuff as a person's fingernails.

Stop and roll!

If a pangolin is scared, it curls up into a ball.

Its tough scales help protect it from **predators**, such as lions.

12

The word *pangolin* means "something that rolls up."

13

Smell that?

A pangolin can!

Pangolins have a strong sense of smell.

Pangolins are great at picking up smells. However, they have poor eyesight.

14

These critters can easily sniff out their favorite foods—ants and termites!

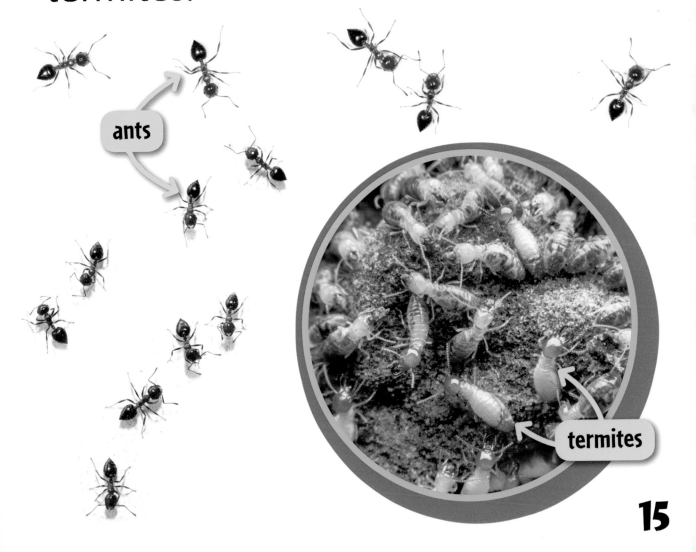

ants

termites

15

Pangolins have long, curved claws on their front feet.

They use their claws to dig for food.

claws

However, these claws make it hard to get around.

So pangolins walk on their knuckles!

a pangolin digging

Pangolins sometimes walk on their hind legs.

17

Slurp, slurp, slurp.

Pangolins have long, sticky tongues.

They poke their tongues into the ground to catch insects.

They eat thousands of bugs each day!

Pangolins don't have any teeth.

Mother pangolins have only one baby at a time.

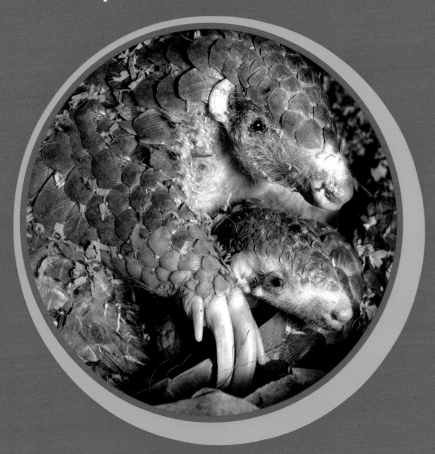

The baby has a special way of getting around.

It rides on its mom's tail!

A baby pangolin is called a pango-pup.

More Strange Scaly Animals

Komodo Dragon

The Komodo dragon is the largest lizard in the world! Don't let its size fool you. These lizards can run up to 13 miles per hour (21 kph)!

Madagascar Leaf-Nosed Snake

This snake's nose looks like a leaf! It lives in trees on an island near Africa. The snake can grow up to 3 feet (1 m) long, and it eats small lizards.

Mudskipper

The mudskipper lives in wet, muddy areas around the world. These strange fish use their front fins like legs to move around on land!

Glossary

armor (AR-mur)
a hard covering that
protects the body

mammals (MAM-uhlz)
warm-blooded animals
that are covered with
hair or fur and drink their
mothers' milk as babies

predators (PRED-uh-turz)
animals that hunt and kill
other animals for food

scales (SKAYLZ) hard
plates that cover the
body of an animal

23

Index

Read More

Blakemore, Victoria. *Pangolins (Elementary Explorers).* Fort Meyers, FL: Victoria Blakemore (2017).

Ricciuti, Edward R. *What on Earth Is a Pangolin?* San Diego, CA: Blackbirch Press (1994).

Learn More Online

To learn more about pangolins, visit
www.bearportpublishing.com/EvenWeirderAndCuter

About the Author

Laura Bryant is a writer and a middle school math and science teacher. She loves learning about weird animals.